PROJECT LEADERSHIP

THE TEN MOST IMPORTANT THINGS YOU
NEED TO BELIEVE

SHANNON KUZMICH

SOUL WORDS

COPYRIGHT

A SOUL WORDS EBOOK/PAPERBACK
First published in the United States in 2020 by Soul Words
eBook first published in 2020 by Soul Words
Copyright © Soul Words 2020

All of the scenarios described in this book are loosely based upon actual events. Any resemblance to actual persons living or dead is purely coincidental.

All rights reserved. No part of this publication may be reproduced, stored in a retrieval system or transmitted in any form or by any means, without the prior permission in writing of the publisher, nor to be otherwise circulated in any form of binding or cover other than that in which it is published without a similar condition, including this condition, being imposed on the subsequent purchaser.

CONTENTS

Why I've Written This Little Book — v

PART I
INTRODUCTION

The Dilemma — 3
Belief 1: It's Not About You … And You Matter — 5
Belief 2: It's Always About the Path Forward — 11

PART II
ABOUT YOU

Belief 3: Integrity is King — 25
Belief 4: Leaders Are Ready to be Lightning Rods — 34
Belief 5: Forgiveness Maintains Momentum — 39

PART III
ABOUT OTHERS

Belief 6: Every Team Member is a Treasure — 45
Belief 7: Openness + Decisiveness Finds the Way — 55

PART IV
ABOUT THE WORK

Belief 8: The Work Takes What It Takes — 63
Belief 9: Effective Leaders Master the Material — 70

PART V
FINAL THOUGHTS

Belief 10: Courageous Leaders Run to the Roar   81

Notes   85
Enjoy this book? You can make a difference   89
Also By …   91
About the Author   95

WHY I'VE WRITTEN THIS LITTLE BOOK

I've written this little book partly to redeem myself, and partly because there are some things in life that remain the same, but are often forgotten.

Redemption

At the height of my career, when I had reached beyond the tipping point of know-how and experience coupled with a wide sphere of influence, I had become a little too full of myself. I wasn't always kind. I was rarely patient. And I flunked the course on work/life balance, leaving my husband to deal with the extraordinary needs of our two kids. I have no regrets given the circumstances at the time, but I now see the impact of my mental and emotional absence.

Reminder

Humans are funny. We fall for false narratives about ourselves all the time, especially when we've been lulled by the trappings of our success. It's the "I have, therefore, I am" syndrome. No matter how grounded we think we are, those little notions are insidious. They get inside of us, distorting our perspective and pulling our attention away from what's important, including *who we really are*.

It's a Philosophical Take

This book is heavy on the philosophical, and light on the how-to. Why? There are already hundreds of great books available on the how-to of project leadership, and I don't have any qualms with what those books provide. My aim with this book is to lift your perspective up a level or two, and give you a jolt of hopeful inspiration.

This is a book of principles that are ancient, yet remain true. My hope is that you'll consider them in your daily thoughts, that they will find their way into your heart, and continuously nourish your soul. May you live more fully in your own integrity, kindheartedness and sense of greater purpose.

About Me

I started working when I was six years old. How else could I still be so young and claim to have accumulated almost 35 years as a professional wrangler of people, processes, and projects?

Not buying it, eh? Yeah, I wouldn't either.

I began my career in the insurance industry as an operations supervisor-turned-operations analyst during the days of Quality Circles and engineered time standards. I was very young, but immediately demonstrated a knack for seeing the big picture, deconstructing it into its functional parts, and understanding what it requires to run as a well-oiled machine.

This ability to *see* systems and read a room of people opened the doors to a rewarding career. From the insurance arena I moved into the utility industry, designing and implementing utility-wide productivity programs and systems. That was my day job.

At night, I spent my hours attending evening courses to earn my undergraduate degree in Social Science (Economics, Sociology, and Psychology). Why Social Science? I wanted to be a lawyer. That is, until I took a prelaw class where we conducted mock trials. It was fascinating to watch the other students battle it out until it was my turn to play the defense attorney. I couldn't do it. I couldn't bring myself to defend someone I knew was guilty. So, I decided to go into consulting. A few short months after graduating, I landed a job working for one of the Big 8 consulting firms (the best one, in my opinion). I had finally found my people! That's when things really took off.

Over the next 25 years, I worked with teams on a variety of engagements for both private and public sector clients, traveled extensively around the world training new staff and new managers how to "do" consulting, served as the regional director of marketing for another Big 6 firm (there were some mergers in the market), joined a small firm that grew into a very successful company that was eventually acquired, and started and ran three of my own firms at various points along the way. Oh … and earned an MBA. The longest chunk of that timeframe was spent chasing contracts and working on large-scale systems development projects that often extended anywhere from four to seven years, employing hundreds of people assigned to teams spread across multiple locations.

A few years ago, I had a brief conversation with the daughter of a friend who was interested in going into the profession. She wanted my advice.

So, I started rattling off a laundry list of concepts, and as I did, her eyes grew wide and her smile even wider.

She said, "You should write a book!"

So, I did.

PART I

INTRODUCTION

THE DILEMMA

The best laid project plans look great when presented by a cadre of smartly dressed and articulate consultants. But plans are rarely executed in perfect adherence to the original vision. It's impossible. Just like life, projects are unpredictable, unruly, sometimes sickly, sometimes healthy, and always dependent upon people. So, why plan?

You have to start somewhere.

You *can* come very close to hitting the plan's milestones, but not without having completed a rigorous planning process. Unfortunately, the opportunity to do that rigorous planning is rare. Here's why:

Clients tend to set the completion date before the planning begins. And here's what happens:

- The project planners are forced to cut the suit out to fit the cloth;
- Which means the suit won't fit the work;
- Unless you put the work on a diet;
- And if you don't put the work on a diet, you'll need to make the required alterations.

It's that simple. But your client won't understand this whole inevitability of deviation from plan problem. And if they do, they'll behave as if they don't. They consider it to be "holding the line." It's a good thing to do, but only to a certain extent. To what extent?

To the extent that the client trusts in the abilities of the project manager. And you, as the project manager, must earn that trust.

This still may not fix the initial planning foible, but having the client's trust sure can help when it's time to make those tricky alterations. With a little trust, a dash of creativity, and a lot of experience, you can successfully build a creative and committed problem-solving team that won't be stopped.

On that note, let's get to it.

BELIEF 1: IT'S NOT ABOUT YOU … AND YOU MATTER

> You as a person have a much greater impact on others than you will ever fully know.

Humans are complicated. Driven by temperament, fears, beliefs, assumptions, and needs, we can really make a mess of things.

Project organizations are like a miniature ecosystem of humans trying to work together to get something done. The main difference is that a project is temporary, with a defined beginning and end. Of course, all projects have a middle, but not everyone can see it at the start, which is why the world has project managers.

Here's another way to look at it. A project organization is like a small city. No, it's not like a company, although similar, I'll give you that. I prefer the city metaphor because a project often brings in different groups of outsiders into the client organization to do some type of specialized work. They're like a diverse group of visitors representing different countries who've come together in a particular city for a brief stay. Outsiders, or non-client staff, serve on the project for a defined period of time to fulfill a contract obligation. Their allegiance is to their employer or to themselves first, and to the client second. It's not a bad thing. It's just something a project manager has to understand. Especially a project manager who is also a temporary visitor.

Other than that, the analogy of building a temporary company to support the workings and lifecycles of a project is a pretty good one. It's definitely better to sort these things out in the planning stage rather than run headlong into issues as the needs arise later on. If you don't, they'll come back to bite you, hindering the project's momentum. And then you'll have some explaining to do.

So, think about the project as a small city of misaligned locals and visitors that need to collaborate as if they were a unified community (organization, processes, tools, policies, and protocols). And then remember that there will always be subversive countercultures working to meet their own agendas because of their first allegiances. It's reality.

Makes you want to be a project manager, right?

Yes? Great, let's continue.

This chapter is about self-awareness.

Let's imagine you've just joined a project that's been underway for some time. Maybe you're not the project manager in title yet, but you are by nature. You think like a project manager. You see things that others don't see. You anticipate where things might be headed. To you, the gaps are glaring, and you want to fix them. But you've just arrived.

Don't start making friends and influencing people by pointing out that the dog is ugly.

Remind yourself that you're in learning mode. You're a sponge with a smile and an open ear. And you're meeting the people, the most important moving part of the project.

So, let's get to the point of this first chapter.

It's not about you.

And you matter.

It's Not About You

You may see yourself as a highly competent professional, respected by your peers, and on a successful career trajectory. Good for you, but the fact remains: your role as a project manager is not about you.

> "The potential success of the project is dependent upon the potential of the team."

I know. It's hard getting out from behind your own needs, wants, and desires; not to mention all the childhood baggage you're still carrying around from project to project. Set all of that aside. Do whatever you have to do: operate out of denial, go to a therapist, seek guidance through prayer, become a fitness fanatic ... do whatever you need to do to get your mind off yourself and focused on the people in front of you.

The people in front of you: see them, see who they are, see their gifts and talents, what motivates them, how they learn, the way they communicate, their body language; anything that will school you on the organizational culture and the team's potential for success. This is important. The potential success of the project is dependent upon the potential of the team. The potential of the team is dependent upon the potential of the individuals on that team. It's critical that you soak it all in. If you don't, and you remain stuck in "you," you won't get there.

Being "others-focused" will be your biggest difference maker.

You Matter

The client is watching you. The executives, managers, staff, and vendors are taking cues from your words and actions, whether you notice it or not. They're sizing you up. From the speed of your gait as you walk down the hall, to the expression on your face when you're not the one running that important meeting, everything you do and how you behave is being scrutinized. What you say, how you say it, whether you say it or not, what you wear, and how you spend your lunch hour are all fair game.

You're building a real time track record. Part of building that track record is to pay attention, affirm, anticipate, and say the things that need to be said in a way that makes it safe for others to open up honestly about the issues that prevent them from doing their job. Work the problems, don't point the fingers, and, most importantly, stay out of the politics. When the team recognizes that you're there for the work (for them) and not for yourself, they'll step up to new and greater challenges. Remember … safe environment. "Problems need to be solved," not "People need to be blamed."

Do your part: serve and respect the team, strive to meet the team members where they're at, and help them to remove the obstacles that are keeping them from fulfilling their responsibilities.

It's not about you ... and you matter.

BELIEF 2: IT'S ALWAYS ABOUT THE PATH FORWARD

> Choose well when determining which path to take.

Now you're the project manager. Wow, isn't that something? Someone had enough confidence in your abilities to place you in the pivotal role of project strategist, project planner, and project driver. It's a big thing, but don't let it go to your head. If you do, you won't be as effective.

This might seem counterintuitive, especially for overachievers who are accustomed to getting results, but if it becomes "about you," your perspective will become muddied. Maintaining a proper perspective takes work.

This chapter is about wisdom; the importance of seeking wisdom and acting wisely within the context of your role as a project manager. Wisdom enables you to anticipate and see the path forward, to communicate it clearly, and to lead the client and the client's team to the final destination.

Every project starts with a picture of the overarching goal painted in bright colors and framed by glorious benefits. It's an exciting time. Your client dreams about how much better the organization will be, and not just in terms of the organization's newly built capacity and strength. They also have expectations about how the project's success will impact their career. On Day-One, they'll be standing at the starting line, gazing off into the future at the finish line, admiring their future selves, affirmed and promoted as a reward for their accomplishments.

Little do they know how much their leadership and character will be tested under the pressure of a multi-year engagement. And that their choices will be proven either as insightful and wise, or short-sighted and foolish, with all the gradations in-between.

Your job is to guide them through the project's ups and downs so that, when all is done, they are better for the journey.

Wisdom Defined

Having wisdom is more than having strong ethics or high moral values. Wisdom is competence with regard to the complex realities of life. It's having the capacity of informed discipline, discernment born out of experience, and a measured discretion that consistently chooses wisely. It's also knowing the right thing to do at the right time in the majority of life situations where ethics and moral values don't apply. In other words, wisdom guides decisions when choices aren't necessarily immoral or unethical, but could be foolish (or less wise) within the context of the specific circumstances. It's something like identifying the good, better, and best choices, but recognizing that *terrible* is also a category on the list.

Why Wisdom is Essential to the Job

A project manager's job is to derive order out of chaos, and then work to sustain that order even as the project navigates the rougher patches along the road. Keeping the project destination in view at all times is essential for so many reasons. First, it seems to have a mysterious psychological effect on the collective, aligning both conscious and subconscious intentions toward a single focal point of success.

Second, seeing the destination is necessary to getting started on the right foot, and honestly, it's fun to place a pushpin on a map and dream of crossing the finish line.

With the collective attention focused on the destination, your job is to ensure there's a thoughtful plan for getting there. Do you hitchhike, or fly the Concorde? Do you hire a guide, or do you attempt the journey with only a compass? Do you need to buy travel gear, research train schedules, book hotels, pack provisions for emergencies, or arrange for guides to meet you along the way? What about the fitness of the travelers? Are they ready? And what about travel insurance? Oh, and what about global instability? Could there be any threats along the way, and if so, how do you prepare? These are the kinds of questions that keep the declining number of travel agents busy in a world of online travel services.

Now think about your project. Newsflash: it will be much harder than planning and mapping out a trip to Paris. Why? Because there will be tens and possibly hundreds of mini-journeys along the way, depending upon the size of the overall project effort. And guess what? The project manager is on point to anticipate and map out the mini-journeys along the way, and then accommodate the inevitable disruptions to the original plan without losing time in getting to the final destination.

You're the Han Solo of the project, charged with flying the Millennium Falcon through the asteroid storms without getting shot down.

That's not going to be possible in every case, but it's certainly your going-in position. It's like a "make it work moment," the encouragement [1]Tim Gunn offers when a frantic designer is walking behind a model who's wearing a dress with half the hem hanging down in the back.

When the inevitable happens (which of course you're ready for with a good schedule, issue and risk tracking processes), it's important to remember, that it's not about you. But you matter.

You don't need to be a hero; just do your work.

What do I mean by "do your work?" You're the one with a big picture management mind who's closest to the subterranean work. When it's time to act (this is where discernment plays its role), do the homework, involve the key stakeholders, get creative, and develop the "make it work" options. Brief your client, asking them to choose which "make it work" option to implement and then update the team using the standard team communication processes (which you implemented at the start of the project and have been using since Day-1). Execute. Lather, rinse and repeat.

As the project gets into an issue-annihilating groove, you'll begin to recognize which macro-activities need closer attention to keep the project on course. The subterranean level is where you'll find the many mini-journeys that are affecting those macro-activities. It's dynamic, unpredictable, and it's where you get your hands into the details. It's also where you'll gain the most leverage in impacting the macro level for the good. Don't back off; these mini-journeys are where the rubber meets the road, and from time to time, you'll need to do a deep dive.

Don't worry about micromanaging. You won't need to be in your team's business all the time; only when there's an issue that requires some extra support. The point is this: pay attention to both the big picture and subterranean levels, understanding and managing the links between them.

Things to Keep in Mind

Hold Onto Wisdom

Remember what you learn. Take hold of wisdom and don't let go. Check in with yourself frequently. Check your motives, fears, concerns, and what's distracting you. Allow wisdom to bring clarity to your perspective. There are no shortcuts. Keep going.

Avoid Foolish Paths

You might assume that this is a no-brainer, but believe me, I've worked with a lot of different people, and this needs to be said. We're human and we're susceptible to the persuasions of "opportunities" that fuel the desire for something we think we need. Sometimes it's job security or power. Sometimes it's ego. Regardless, in your role as project manager, you're going to run into some pretty nasty stuff. People will lie to you, try to manipulate you, and some will even try to take you down. Don't get yanked off course and start following a path that will only get you deeper into the mire of obscurity that your client hired you to keep them out of.

Bottom line: Don't take a foolish path. Avoid it, pass it by, or even leave the situation if necessary. It's always better to quickly pivot away from a foolish path before you get too far down the road and the damage cannot be undone.

Consider Human Nature

Whatever you think about human potential, it goes both ways. We humans are complex creatures. We tend to absorb and carry the hurts, wounds, and habits from our formative years, and bring them into our adult lives, including our professional lives. You need to know this. What you perceive about a person is only the surface. Most people are a little broken inside.

The good news is that human beings have a mysterious potential to overcome adversity, receive healing, and grow beyond the limitations of their emotional, spiritual, and psychological baggage. Some of us see this and are more intentional about helping ourselves, allowing us to enter into a fuller experience of our lives.

Then there are those who are overcome by brokenness, remaining stuck in dysfunction. They may even recognize their own problems, yet seem helpless to do anything. This is heartbreaking, especially if you believe in the incredible potential each of us carries deep inside.

Finally, there are those of us in between the broken and the helped who haven't dealt with the baggage, but have managed to develop sophisticated coping mechanisms and ways of "being" that help us find our safe places in life. That was me.

My point is this: We're all on a journey.

Be empathetic.

And do your best to exercise discernment. When it comes to managing a project, you're dealing with a great deal more than the apparent. You'll run into humans and their stuff every day.

To help you avoid getting distracted or bogged down, consider setting some personal policies that fit who you are and allow you to manage your own baggage.

Here are mine:

1. Know who your client executive is and follow the communications and management protocols they set for you.
2. Be trustworthy, maintain all confidences, and politely avoid participating in gossip. I've had many clients who loved to gossip, but I never engaged. Granted, my avoidance made them uncomfortable, but eventually they understood I could be trusted with the reputation of others … and theirs.
3. Acknowledge and show respect to all team members. This can be difficult, especially with those client staff who would like nothing better than to have the role you've been hired into. But do it anyway. Most of the time, you will win them over as they recognize that you're there to make them successful.
4. Focus on navigating the path forward.
5. Stay out of the politics.
6. Take things at face value and act on what was agreed upon until there's a formal

change. Even though your instincts will tell you when someone is trying to manipulate the circumstances, it's not your job to meddle in client dynamics.
7. When a project issue arises, focus on solving the problem, not blaming the person(s).
8. Work hard, meet the team where they are and help them to the extent they need help to get the job done. In other words, don't hesitate to get your hands dirty.
9. Play your part in creating a safe team environment where honest communication can safely occur, and the team can be more productive.

Clarity Offers the Clues

You cannot manage what you cannot see.

You *must* create and maintain a clear and accurate picture of overall project progress. It will enable you to keep the target visible, quickly identify issues, and drill down into the details to find the root of any deviations from plan.

Look Outward and Listen

Finally, regardless of how much experience you have, each project will have its own personality, including strengths, weaknesses, and blind spots.

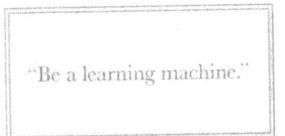

Be a learning machine: learn the project dynamics, study the map of the path forward, and keep your eyes open for signs that it's time to pivot the team into a new phase. That's the thing about projects: they change over time, which means the project's organization chart will change, as it should. It's your job to anticipate and get in front of each phase, and prepare your client for what needs to happen in order to hit the ground running once the subsequent phase begins.

PART II

ABOUT YOU

Don't be confused. It's still not about you. But you're still you. Part II is about you as a person in the role of project leader.

BELIEF 3: INTEGRITY IS KING

> When the winds start blowing, a whole person weathers the storm.

I've often bristled at the remark, "It's just business." When the person sitting behind the desk in front of me utters those awful words of doom, I know they will eventually betray my trust. It may not be a huge betrayal. There are plenty of things we forgive of one another with a wink and a nod along with an implied IOU. But the small things are only the tip of the iceberg. Betrayals of great consequence are always born out of the lesser ones once sealed with a wink and a nod. The IOU never sticks.

A person's conscious choice to try and work the system, manipulating protocols or processes to their advantage, is always foolish. The foolish think they're savvy or clever, someone to be reckoned with: a hard-nosed business person ... a winner. After all, everyone does it, right? It's the only way to get to the top.

I don't think so.

Greed Kills the Spirit

If I've learned anything about human behavior it's this: We are frighteningly capable masters at justifying our own otherwise despicable behavior under the banner of "It's just business." This is especially true if we've achieved success and, as a result, are enjoying some very nice financial rewards. We would never consider ourselves to be greedy. We're just special, and of course we're generous, especially when we want something.

When a person starts making more money than they've ever dreamed, it's easy for them to start believing that they're above: above others ... above morality ... above the law. Their identity becomes tied to their bank account, and they grow increasingly blind to how poorly they treat other people they see as beneath them.

What does this have to do with project management? A great deal.

Greed is insidious. It distorts perspective and hinders judgment. A once clear focus takes a hard left away from the all-important work, and instead starts chasing after the seat of power (or wealth, or influence) within the organization. The work suffers, the frequency of "blaming over solving" increases, the project slows to a crawl, and [1]CYA becomes the new mode of management.

You get the point. If you allow yourself to be pulled into the race for money and power, you'll stop sleeping at night, lose your credibility with the teams, and eventually suffer the inevitable consequences.

What's the solution?

Stay focused on the job. It's not about you. Strive to remain in your integrity, no matter the situation or consequences.

Integrity Under Pressure

A person of integrity is *one and whole,* and not at all duplicitous. They don't use phrases like, "It's just business." To a person of integrity, it's *all* personal, and not in that touchy-sensitive way. It's *all* personal in a way that values the truth, behaves honestly, and respects others.

Project managers often face tests of their integrity; there may be tremendous pressure to bend to the will

> "To a person of integrity, it's all personal."

of others. Against that pressure, integrity stands firm. I've found that myself tested on many occasions and my best stance has always been honest transparency. A project leader is better off pursuing wholeness for the long run rather than convenience in the moment. It's a process, so don't be too hard on yourself.

Expect Hostility

You as a project manager will encounter hostility. Be ready for it and be tough, but don't be a jerk. You'll find that when you do your job and do it well, the organization might be exposed. Not everyone appreciates someone else airing their dirty laundry. This could lead them to direct hostility toward you.

Stay the course; be gracious and remain diligent. You'll find that there are many who will come alongside in support of your trustworthiness, honesty, and work ethic. Accept that not everyone is going to like you.

Diligence Isn't Enough

Diligence will take you a long way, especially through multi-year projects. But that won't be enough. If you endeavor to maintain your integrity out of self-interest, it will not hold you up over the long haul. If the only motivation for your honesty is fear, then you'll be dishonest in situations where you're afraid of being found out.

It's important to reflect upon your own motives, especially when things get tough. Motives rooted in insecurity may lead to behaviors that are counterproductive or that negatively impact others. From time to time, circumstances will get rough, and we humans often resort to survival mode tactics without even thinking about it. Try to stay mindful of what's going on within your own thoughts and emotions, exercise a little healthy self-talk, and endeavor to stay the course.

Stay on Top of the Details

Up until the early 2000s I worked with people who really loved the actual work. Each morning we arrived at the office or client site ready to hit the ground running. Why? Because we had a clear goal, we supported each other, and we had each other's backs. On top of that, our bosses were never hesitant to dive in when we needed the extra muscle. We worked hard and did good work, and because of that, we were often asked by our clients to stay and do more good work. It seemed simple.

Then, in 2002, while working as part of a multi-company proposal effort, one of the young consultants from one of the other companies remarked, "I'm not used to working with managers who actually do work."

His words struck me as odd. I was puzzled. I had always taken it for granted that anyone who wore the consultant's uniform, regardless of position in the hierarchy, was ready to jump in whenever he or she was needed.

Little did I know that his words marked an oncoming change to my work culture.

The young man was right. I saw for myself that the *best and brightest* in his organization were ten levels above him, and none of them had a clear understanding of what was going on at the client level. The executives didn't get involved in the actual client work, but instead seemed to spend considerable time creating new methods of exerting power over the many levels of staff below them. They frequently required staff to run administrative fire drills, taking valuable consulting time away from delivering client work. It may, in their minds, have been worth the investment of time, but from my perspective those fire drills often had little to do with improving the capacity of the company to deliver client services. I assumed the executives had once been young consulting stars, but something had gotten into them.

They no longer showed the interest they once had. They were no longer available to help. They no longer stayed abreast of the issues the teams in the trenches were dealing with. They had put themselves at an unhealthy distance from the people and work they were responsible for managing. It was too bad. As a result, I recall repeatedly hearing about other client engagements that had suffered for lack of needed executive support.

> "Stay connected with the details of the work."

Don't be like those higher-ups. Stay connected with the details of the work, remain close to your team leads, get to know the team members, and ask questions to learn about the technical issues they're dealing with. Act when needed to support their efforts. It will take time: you'll spend a significant portion of your days following email threads to ensure that progress continues, interjecting to unclog logjams, and advocating for the project with executive management when their support is needed to keep things on track.

You see, if you're focusing on the work, all the other great things will happen in due course. Those responsible with a little are usually given more.

Speaking Truth to Power

Speaking of management, an important part of your role is to report progress to executive management, including deviations from the plan. Maybe you've looked forward to the next set of activities and discovered a red flag. You've done some analysis and discovered that major adjustments need to be made to avoid a negative schedule impact. And you know that the implications of your analysis won't be well received.

Before you walk into the client's office, make sure you've developed a thoughtful solution. One cardinal rule of maintaining project momentum is to never, ever, allow the project to fall into "problem-admiration" mode. Problem-admiration mode happens when an issue emerges, the teams seeks to understand it, people talk about it … a lot, and yet there's no movement forward in developing a resolution. This sometimes happens if there's a gap in the lines of responsibility and problem ownership, a gap that isn't always immediately evident until someone (the project manager or leader) starts asking questions.

Whatever issues you report must be coupled with a proposal for resolving them, or at least a plan for developing a proposal that will resolve them. Keep the focus on moving forward. You don't get to just dump the issues on the table and walk away. Your job is to facilitate progress, not allow the engine to stall.

The executives understand that detecting problems is part of your job. Yes, things will sometimes turn political; they won't always be happy with the news. Once in a while, you may ruffle a few feathers. It's unavoidable, but I've found that if the issues are presented fully and transparently, avoiding all hints of finger-pointing, the executives will recognize that they've been put into the best possible position to make an informed decision.

Be a straight shooter, avoid personalizing the issues, offer thoughtful options for resolution, and never insert yourself into the politics. You're going to have enough natural detractors without complicating the situation by your own doing.

BELIEF 4: LEADERS ARE READY TO BE LIGHTNING RODS

> Lightning rods take the brunt of resistance to the first signs of change on the horizon.

Do you have your armor ready? I hope so because you're going to need it.

One of the reasons you were hired was to make sure the project gets done while shielding your client along the way. Your job is to step out in front of the crowd and call out the issues that everyone else is reluctant to mention.

Yes, I know. It's not all fun and games, but you *can* succeed, and it can be very rewarding. You just need to put on the appropriate suit of armor.

The Consultant's Armor

Helmet of Mindset

At the top of the list is the helmet of mindset. Remember, it's not about you, but you matter. What you say and how you say it, and what you do and how you do it, are tantamount to your long-term effectiveness (and job security), especially when you're in lightning rod mode.

You'll be poking the bear, and the bear doesn't like to be poked. No matter what you're trying to accomplish, there will be someone who is threatened by your actions. Depending upon where they sit in the organization, their response to your efforts will range from a benign resentment that makes your interactions temporarily awkward, all the way to outright sabotage. Believe me, I've been hassled enough times to know when one of the bears is irritated. The claws will come out, looking to give you a little swipe. Expect it.

Now that you're expecting it, watch and learn: be a continuous student of human behavior.
[1]Remember, these are *people* you're working with; individuals who offer value in their current job and who hold out hope for a successful career. If you walk in and threaten to derail their plans, look out. They may act out, but try to remember this: they're not the enemy (even though they may act

like it). There are some exceptions to this; for instance, if you are threatened or assaulted. Threats and assault incidents should be reported immediately, no question about that. Don't worry, it's rare, but it does happen.

Am I scaring you? I don't mean to scare you. I mean to prepare you for the more difficult aspects of the job. So, let's continue.

Personal Integrity

The next piece of armor is your personal integrity. There will be days when you're being treated unfairly, or even lied about. Don't take the bait. Maintain your position, treat everyone with respect, maintain confidences, and don't step out of your role. Remember, again (yes, I'm a broken record), it's not about you. People will notice how you handle tough situations and grow to trust you over time.

A Good Tactical Defense

Finally, the tactical defense parts of the suit. Stay the course in terms of these six things:

1. Always follow the chain of command and communications protocol. There's nothing worse than losing the trust of a key client because you didn't follow protocol.

2. Take things at face value and act. You may suspect that there is more going on than meets the eye, but the only way to keep the project activities moving forward is to confirm and act upon what you've been told by those who have the authority to give you direction.
3. Communicate clearly, completely, and professionally in all verbal interactions and written documents, especially email.
4. Leverage the regularly scheduled status meetings (that you've set up and faithfully facilitate on a regular basis) to keep the status of all project activities visible, understandable, and actionable.
5. Bring light to every issue and risk, and work with the teams to find practical blame-free solutions and mitigation strategies. Show the team your confidence in them, and your respect for them.
6. Don't pull any punches, but make the punches feel like a breath of fresh air. It's like that old adage: *It's not what you say, it's how you say it.*

Finally - Health of Mind and Body

Life works when you work out, eat right, and get enough rest.

Believe me, there have been many a day I awoke with a work hangover from the day before, and I wasn't exactly excited about hitting it hard for the 12th day in a row without a day off. What was (is) my remedy? I get up long before sunrise to spend about an hour in silence and solitude before a hard workout at the gym. It never fails to refresh me for the high-pressure day ahead.

> "Life works when you work out, eat right, and get enough rest."

If you don't have a self-care routine that recharges your mind and body, then get one. You'll thank me later.

BELIEF 5: FORGIVENESS MAINTAINS MOMENTUM

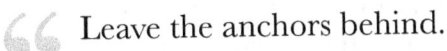 Leave the anchors behind.

Are you a forgiving person? If not, then you should start practicing. If you are, you already know that forgiveness allows a free and steady back and forth flow in your relationships. And at the end of the day, projects are all about people and relationships.

Why is forgiveness so hard? Well, because when someone injures you, and they don't take responsibility for it, there's a cost to you.

Imagine that you are at your friend's house and the doorbell rings. He's busy, so you answer the door to find the postman standing there with a letter marked "postage due." You go ahead and pay the postman yourself. Your friend doesn't pay you back, but it was only a couple of bucks. That's not a big deal, right? You let it go and pay down the debt yourself.

But if you loaned your Maserati to a friend and they totaled it, and then came back to you and said, "Sorry about that, chief," as they handed you the keys before driving off in their crummy Tesla, they'd be leaving you with a much greater cost to absorb.

It could take years to pay off a hit like that.

So, the cost of the injury, the loss, and the hurt cannot be denied. And it must be paid.

The question is this: who pays?

When we don't forgive those who injure us, we're placing the burden of paying the debt on them. You could go after them in court, you might build a wall to keep them at a distance, or you decide to shut down the relationship.

But the unpaid debt is still there. Whether you know it or not, you're actually waiting for them to apologize and make you whole. You're waiting, believing they owe you, all the while standing your ground because, of course, you believe you're justified. Maybe you are.

But it doesn't do any good. You're stuck in time; your life is now defined in part by the terrible thing they did to hurt you. If you still have to be around them, you might not be as available as you once were; you've cooled toward them. You might even feel bitter or cheated. And eventually, over time, your offender becomes only a thin and unredeemable caricature of a real person you once knew.

It will happen. People will fail you. Most of the time, they don't even realize it. Or if they do, they've justified it in their own mind. Regardless of whether there was malice involved or not, you really *can* choose to let it go. How you handle the situation will be determined by your past experience and your understanding of how toxic a lack of forgiveness can be.

Even so.

Get over it. Please. You can't afford to be distracted by the mental baggage of resentment, bitterness, and anger. You've got a job to do, and so do they. And … take a deep breath, it's your job to help them succeed in doing their part.

PART III
ABOUT OTHERS

BELIEF 6: EVERY TEAM MEMBER IS A TREASURE

> Potential is limitless. Lead in a way that sets it free.

A team is made up of individuals. These individuals may combine staff recruited from different parts of the organization with vendors brought in from different companies. They may not know each other at all, may know each other only by reputation, or maybe they've been working together for a while already. The project has brought them into a new work context, and on their first day as a team, they'll begin a journey through the four stages of Tuckman's[1] group development model: Forming, Storming, Norming and Performing. The degree to which the team experiences each stage will vary, but you can bet that all four stages will emerge.

While this is happening, the team members will be searching for their individual spots on the team. As they do, they'll be looking for signals from you to help them navigate each stage. The best thing you can do is to respond in a way that facilitates their progress through the stages. Be generous. It will go a long way in unlocking their potential contributions to the team's success.

Kindness is Essential

Don't bristle. Kindness is not about sappy slogans framed by butterflies and flowers. Kindness is about the quality of your demonstrated attitude toward others. I like the Wikipedia[2] definition best: Kindness is a behavior marked by ethical characteristics, a pleasant disposition, and concern and consideration for others.

"It's not what you say, it's how you say it."[3] That's a bit of practical wisdom I picked up from a car salesman friend I knew way back when. "Words have meaning," is another tidbit I picked up from a former colleague. Her point was that using the appropriate word for the occasion is tantamount to clearly communicating important ideas, concepts, facts, analyses, requests, and expectations. I would also say that *words have impact*. The words you select, and the tone of voice you use in delivering those words, can make a significant difference in how your words are received, and whether you're on track to build a good relationship with that person.

Your manner of speech matters. Your "goal" is that every experience of your project leadership, including how you interact with team members, contributes to the development and maturity of the team, preparing them for the challenges they will meet after you're gone.

Your Speech

Your "speech" is informed by how you look at your world. Insecure project leaders tend to look at their world, including their career, as a zero-sum game competition. They believe success is finite and there's only so much of it to go around. They want it all.

They need to be top dog and are often bent on blocking anyone else from taking their seat on the throne. You'll know it by the vibe you get when they recognize your competence. You'll know it by their body language. You'll know it by how their personalities change depending upon who's in the room. And you'll know it by how little respect they show their fellow team members.

Don't be that guy. You will only stumble at some point, you won't sleep because of your paranoia, and your team won't ever feel they can trust you. Your team needs to trust you, and they want to trust you. Make it easy for them to do that.

Why do I write about this under a section called, "Your Speech?" Because your speech comes out in many ways, not only through words. Your words are important, but your actions and your body language often speak louder. Your team isn't stupid. They may not challenge the bad behavior of a self-centered leader, but believe me, the project's progress will be hindered by an undercurrent of frustration and distrust.

I once facilitated a meeting between the project's engineering team and a subject matter expert for another system potentially impacted by the project. Our invited expert walked in, dragging a dust cloud with him, obviously displeased about something. A few minutes into the meeting, the discussion became a little heated. I suspected he was unhappy that he hadn't been consulted earlier. I started asking questions, trying to surface the real issue so that we could discuss it through to resolution. This time, however, one of the server administrators on the engineering team interrupted me and laid into our visiting expert. Things went downhill fast.

So, what did I do?

Without a second thought, I started singing.

I'm not kidding. I'd just seen a kid's film with my two daughters at the local theatre, and the movie's song about teamwork had been running through my head ever since. I started singing the song … all the way through to its end. You could have heard a pin drop.

And then the smiles broke out. Even the angry expert's body language softened a bit. We then agreed to table the topic and reschedule a smaller group discussion for the following day. The subsequent meeting went much better.

You're a straight talker? That's great; keep that part, but make sure you're delivering your words with

> "Stumbles become opportunities."

a respectful candor. It will be a breath of fresh air, and the team's spirit will be lifted. Stumbles become opportunities. Misunderstandings simply point to where communication protocols and processes need improvement. Mistakes become opportunities to help come alongside those team members who need a little help. Make lemonade out of lemons and be enthused about the opportunities that present themselves. When the team feels supported and that the environment allows for a periodic foible, they'll be motivated to do their best.

Making Things Right

Speaking of making things right, you don't always have to start singing in the middle of a meeting to de-escalate a situation. Humor works too, especially if you're naturally witty. When people are laughing, they're relaxed and more likely to participate in whatever process is underway. Words that tickle the funny bone are "sweet to the soul," bringing healing to the team, the person, and the circumstances. Kind speech heals anxiety, gentle speech (or a spontaneous breaking into song) can extinguish anger and resentment, and candid words can erase ignorance and self-deception.

Humility

Humility is probably one of the most misunderstood and least practiced attitudes amongst humans. After all, many project professionals look at a project role as an opportunity to showcase what they've got, which in turn could lead to a promotion, another contract, more money, and a strong reputation. You ought to have confidence in yourself to be effective, right?

Be careful.

If you look up the definition of "humility" in the dictionary, you'll get some-

Belief 6: Every Team Member is a Treasure

> "Humility is ...
> the maturity and experience to see things as they are."

thing that uses comparison and hierarchy as a measuring stick. I don't agree with this definition. I'd like to make the case for the word "humility" to be defined as the maturity and experience to see things as they are, not as we wish them to be, imagine them to be, fantasize them to be, or are purported to be by others. *As they are*, including your own capabilities, talents, strengths, and most importantly, your weaknesses. You absolutely cannot effectively lead without humility. Why? Because you won't be willing to see the talents and gifts of others. Why is that important?

You've got a project to run and a result to deliver.

You will exponentially improve your chance of succeeding as a project manager by first seeing and then drawing out the treasures of talents, skills, and gifts possessed by the individuals and collective teams working within the scope of your management control.

Bottom line: your job is to facilitate the development of excellence in others.

But hold on a second.

A good leader also has the ability to assess the character of others. If you can't read people's hearts and winnow out those who only intend to disrupt and undermine the team's progress, you won't manage well. Either naïveté or cynicism about people—habitually over-trusting or under-trusting motivations—will hinder your effectiveness as a project manager.

Discerning important nuances isn't done by following a methodology.

Manners

When I was growing up in what was then the Big Eight consulting environment, some of the female staff (this was in the 80s) seemed to think it necessary to be rude and abrasive to get the attention they thought they deserved. They got the attention all right; along with a reputation for being rude and abrasive. Their behavior, although aiming to prove their competence and capability on par with the guys, ended up squelching the other members of the team, hindering the team's ability to freely communicate and work together.

Order matters. Okay, I know some of you are little rebels like me, but think about the others for a moment. And now for another moment think about how much more open team members can be when they know the environment is one that encourages the sharing of ideas, and values courtesy and respect for one another.

You and your team members will benefit from adherence to common codes of behavior in order to prevent team life from becoming abrasive, unpleasant, and unsafe. Polite company and basic courtesy can go a long way. Expectations and norms will vary across company cultures, but here are some examples of simple professional courtesies:

- Be prepared for and on time to meetings;
- Respond to email and other types of messages in a timely manner;
- Communicate work status clearly and completely;
- Deliver completed staff work;
- Refrain from using harsh or profane language, and
- Dress in accordance with professional norms. It's a show of respect for the people you work with … and the people you work for.

Power Comes and Goes

Now we're ready to talk about power.

You will have it.

Sometimes you'll have more than you should, and more than you want. Your client will sometimes use you like a lightning rod, and at other times a shield. You're going to take a few hits. It's a part of the job.

And then there'll be times when your power is stripped from you for no apparent or stated reason, but you'll know why, and you'll need to accept it as a part of the job.

Regardless of the ever-shifting degrees of power resting in the office of the project manager, you will always need a solid and stable foundation upon which to stand. What is that? Well, even a king's leadership must be characterized by a love for his people that is evident to them. That is, the team must see that in the end, the project manager would sacrifice him or herself for them, rather than sacrifice them to save him or herself.

> "The most powerful kind of leader is one who ultimately uses his or her authority to serve the ones being led."

The most powerful kind of leader is one who ultimately uses his or her authority to serve the ones being led. The greatest leaders are the greatest servants. But the most powerful leaders are those whom people trust so much that they want to follow them.

BELIEF 7: OPENNESS + DECISIVENESS FINDS THE WAY

> Moving forward means making the call.

Ideas can be exciting.

Sometimes.

Humans have a penchant for control. They don't always like it when people want to draw outside the authorized lines. But guess what? Project managers often need to draw outside the lines to keep things moving forward.

Here's the dilemma: to be successful, the project must innovate. To stay out of trouble, the project must abide by the policies and protocols of the organization. Those two things don't always work hand in hand.

Let's say you and your team are doing all right, but everyone knows that it could be better with a few changes. You know that a brainstorming session with the right people at the table will extract some great ideas from the team's collective mind.

> "Be witness to what happens when a team of individuals discovers the synergies of their collective creativity."

You've seen it before. Give a group of smart people permission to entertain alternative ways of doing things, and look out. Big things start happening. Not only will obstacles be removed, new and clever methods surmised, and deadlines beaten by a long shot, but you'll also be witness to what happens when a team of individuals discovers the synergies of their collective creativity. They start to bond, the overall enthusiasm level goes up, and they move into high-performance mode. All of that is good.

What does this have to do with the value of an open and decisive mind? It has everything to do with it. Your decisions will only be as strong as the ideas upon which they are based. And those ideas need to come from the "A" team. Being open-minded is one thing. Filling that open mind with solid ideas is another. To get to that, all the best players need to be at the table.

So, the first step is to assemble the "A" team.

Gathering the Best Ideas

The Two Organizations

In my experience, there are at least two organizations in every one organization chart. There's the one organization of official hierarchy and functional boundaries with clear mission statements and job descriptions. And then there's the shadow organization that gets most of the mission-critical work done.

You probably know about the 80-20 rule. 80% of the critical work gets done by 20% of the staff. This is important to recognize; the 20% are often the innovators who know how to make things happen. You need to know who they are. Why? Because you want them to fill a seat at the table. The good news is that the team knows who the relevant 20-percenters are. Following the proper protocols, it's a good idea to extend to each of them an invitation to the table.

> "There are at least two organizations in every one organization chart."

Your team also knows that whatever emerges from the table will have to be blessed by the organizational policy folks. The team probably knows who their assigned policy folks are, and it can't hurt to invite a representative to offer their input. They may even have a few ideas of their own, plus they might serve as an advocate for the project when you need to request that a policy exemption be granted.

Do you see where this is leading? I'll spell it out.

> "Find the organization's creative elasticity and tolerance for innovation, and then work within those norms."

You're building an extended team of core members, subject matter experts, and advocates for the effort. You don't need to "cowboy" it (I've seen this happen many times and it's never been good).

Find the organization's creative elasticity and tolerance for innovation and work within those norms, all the while building a strong and well-connected team.

Pursuing Decisions

The extended team has come up with some innovative ideas. And now a series of decisions will need to be considered. Some of the decisions can be considered quickly, such as the ones you've already been authorized to decide upon. Some will take a little more time, but are still within reach, meaning that the decision-maker is already a supporter of the effort and works in close proximity to the work. And then there will be those that require a series of hoop jumps, which could take some time.

Two things to keep in mind. First, there's an order in which to pursue the green lights, beginning with you. Second, you may decide "no" to the proposed idea and send the team back to the drawing board. As part of your own due diligence, you might find an issue with the idea that nullifies its value. It happens all the time. Being an open-minded manager is a good thing, but as someone once said, you ought not to be so open-minded that your brains fall out.

Informed decisiveness will save you from wallowing in 'problem admiration syndrome.' It will also prevent you from taking a lesser path. The difference could be in you, but it depends. Are you "open-minded" because you want people to think well of you? If that's the case, you're going to be reticent to make a decision for fear of appearing autocratic. You need to get past that.

People want to be led by competent leaders they respect. Teams respect a leader who listens, learns, and then makes a considered and informed decision. The project requires that kind of leadership to succeed, and there's nothing like the rush of adrenaline that fuels a team's momentum in executing a new course of action the team itself has come up with.

Making the Call

Making the call is tantamount to sounding the starting gun. Create a plan for executing the implementation of the ideas, including how the consensus building and approvals process are expected to unfold. Keep the team updated, enlist their help and support, ensure that the proper documentation, when required, is clean and complete, and begin meeting with the stakeholders and decision-makers to gain their support.

Finally, capture the activities in the project schedule. This legitimizes the work in a way that allays any concerns about the team going rogue. You've gone to great lengths to involve the right people early on. Getting all green lights is a good thing, so don't drop the ball on the fundamentals.

Owning Bad Decisions

Some decisions don't always lead to the intended result. Own it, learn from it, make amends, forgive, and look for opportunities to do things differently next time. And remember, the client doesn't owe you anything. You serve at their pleasure. Do your job, do it well, and let the chips fall.

You'll be okay.

PART IV

ABOUT THE WORK

BELIEF 8: THE WORK TAKES WHAT IT TAKES

> It's not only about how much of the work is done. It's also about how well the work is done.

I've always had a need to be the fastest in everything I do, including typing and playing the piano. Mozart would turn over in his grave. I've only recently learned the value of being patient with the work. I think of it as letting the work have its voice. Seriously! The work will speak to you if you're willing to get your ear close enough to hear it.

> "My work asks me to pay closer attention, attend to the deeper aspects, and pursue any loose ends."

My work these days asks me to pay closer attention, attend to the deeper aspects of its complex nature, and not dismiss the nagging doubts about the loose ends I doubt anyone else will likely notice. Do something! Go back and see what those doubts are telling you about the work and about your craft. When you're working, you're also learning.

When you're planning a project, give the work a chance to tell you what it's going to take to do it well. Don't under-schedule the work and rely on heroics to hit a deadline. No one does their best work after five straight days of 14-hour shifts. Of course, I recognize that it's done all the time. In fact, the big firms often put their staff through a kind of boot camp, conditioning them to live lives of 80-hour work weeks (I know, because I went through a rigorous boot camp myself). But even though everybody does it, that doesn't make it right. It leads to staff and team burnout, amongst other life-impacting consequences.

Resist the temptation to under budget a project just to get a contract or meet a politically derived deadline. I know; it's unheard of. That's why the client hires people like you and firms like that. But you need to try to bring reason to the plan. If you don't, you won't get any of the additional room you know you will need.

Look at this way. You're becoming a sort of artisan. Take the work seriously. It may take more time than the client would like, but the teams will become better artisans of their craft, enabling them to hit the ball out of the park as their skills and efficiencies reach new levels. The benefits going forward will be worth it to the individuals pursuing their own careers, and to the organization that has effectively bolstered their own capacity to successfully execute big projects.

This chapter addresses what project managers can do to support their teams and lead them across the finish line. It's more than polished messaging and inspirational speeches.

Staying Close to the Work Keeps Things on Course

Ready for a shock? Most projects fail.

Yes, shock of shocks, it's true.

Every project runs into rough patches. After you have a few engagements under your belt, you'll have a sense of when the project will hit the next one. You can't stop it from happening; it's the nature of the beast. But you can prepare for it.

One of the more common reasons projects run into briar patches is this: the project leadership has taken their eyes off the work. And in some cases, they never had their eyes on the work in the first place. You're the gap filler; it's your job to keep everyone's eyes on the work.

This brings us to the first axiom of effective project management:

> "You can't manage what you can't *see*."

The ability to see the project requires that you, the project manager, create and sustain a continuous state of visibility into the most significant project health indicators (i.e., schedule, issues, risks, costs). Whatever way you decide to establish this window into the project truth, it will be the cornerstone of your management toolkit.

The second axiom is this:

> "What you see determines the path forward."

Executives often feel they're being handed a fairytale narrative (understandably so) about how well things are going. Providing decision-makers with a clear picture of how things are *really* going is of great value. As executives, they are better informed, comfortably in control, and willing to throw their support behind the project. Executive support is like gold for the teams. Don't treat it lightly. Your job as the project manager is to inform and educate the executives about the problem, explain their options for remediation, and facilitate the building of consensus around the path forward. This takes work.

To do this well, you must stay focused on what's happening at all levels of the project. Don't get

> "Give executives what they need to support the teams: a clear picture of how things are really going."

distracted. Don't be a de facto delegator, especially when it comes to critical path activities and anything else that those activities are dependent upon. Stay in touch. It's not realistic to think you can delegate and leave key decisions to the team leads, or simply hire any contractor off the street and put them into a back room to do their thing. It's also not fair; they don't have the breadth of perspective that you have.

Diligence is Not Reluctant

Unexpected issues pop up on every project. It's a normal part of project life. I always found it rewarding (and fun) to jump into a brainstorming session with the team leads and a few 20-percenters to hammer out a plan that promises to crush the problem like a bug.

Yet, it doesn't *always* go that way. Sometimes problems are bigger than anything a group of team leads can tackle. And that's where you need to step up.

You see it coming, like a freight train without a headlight, cloaked in a darkness that hides the ferocity of its inevitably destructive impact on the project. You're alone in your ability to see it, and no one else, your client included, wants to believe your tale of doom. Even the team leads come to you in protest, pleading with you to let them try ... doing their best to persuade you that they can get the job done. But your gut, your experience, and the numbers don't support the team's flimsy hopes. You know you're right. And it's your job to keep things on track (no pun intended).

So, what do you do?

First, set aside any notions that you're going to keep your job.

Second, prepare your argument in an executive consumable format.

And third, walk with confidence and poise into the cage, armed with facts, rationale, and the voice of experience.

Be the professional that you are, take all questions and concerns, and don't give up.

> "Walk with confidence and poise into the cage, armed with facts, rationale, and the voice of experience."

Thankfully, I've only found myself in this position a few times, but those few times were pretty big deals. The situations were stressful, but I worked the process, and the train of doom was effectively derailed. Here's why:

1. I offered a strong argument that could not be disputed.
2. I was willing to allow the client to use me as their shield (scapegoat).
3. I was prepared to lose my job.

In all of those situations, I'd been hired to help turn a failing project around, a fact that made it easier to deal with the nasty challenge. I was doing what they'd hired me to do.

Even so, no one wants to hear that their dog is ugly. I found a few residual feathers on the floors from the ruffling I'd done, but they all kept me on.

And the freight trains were stopped.

The point is this: be diligent, keep your eyes on the project, and don't get distracted by any fears you might entertain about the impact on your role or status. It's not about you.

BELIEF 9: EFFECTIVE LEADERS MASTER THE MATERIAL

> Don't be a half-empty suit. Become a discerning expert.

This chapter is about bringing your experience to bear in developing strategies and plans that take all things into consideration for the benefit of the entire project.

It's also about not throwing the baby out with the bathwater.

I'll use an analogy. I highly recommend using analogies. They will help you make things clear when talking with your team, your key client staff, and your executive steering committee. But don't overdo it.

The best presenters are those who have mastered their material. Why? Because they're not just parroting what someone told them in a course, or what they might have read in a book. They're demonstrating their command of the concepts studied early on in their career, coupled with their experience in applying those concepts over time. You can tell that they've ridden in a few rodeos, and at this point, they've internalized the typical patterns of project life. Their gut is now fine-tuned to give them a nudge when those pesky signs of trouble start popping up.

As an audience member, you "know" a presenter who has got the goods and the one who's winging it, right? Presenters with the goods can take any and all questions without blinking. They're quick on their feet as they instantaneously draw from a good-sized reservoir of knowledge and experience. Not to mention they've done their homework ... themselves.

The presenters who are "winging it" read from the slides, don't look at the audience, and can't answer questions without shooting a desperate glance to their manager, who is usually the one they're trying to impress. Well, maybe that sounds too cynical. I was that person too when I first started ... once. After that first mortifying episode (my throat closed up and I couldn't speak), I started investing the needed time in preparation.

Your job is to master the material, in this case having a comprehensive grasp of the project activities (including the interplay of workload, staffing levels/skillsets, and scheduling), the adequacy of the project facilities, any critical technological dependencies, any issues or risks associated with using outside vendors, the current organizational expectations and policies, and most importantly, where the project is on the overall journey toward completion.

See? It's not that much. Of course, I'm obviously referring to huge projects that go on for many months, and oftentimes years. But smaller projects of shorter durations still have many of the same components, only on a much smaller scale. And honestly, smaller and shorter projects can be harder to manage because they move across phases at a faster rate, which means the team may not have enough time to get into a groove that offers a sustained momentum.

Yet, don't be discouraged. If you've mastered the material, you know how to set up a short-term project for success.

The Value of Methodologies

Let's talk about methodologies for a moment. Methodologies are good, as long as you recognize them for what they are. First, a methodology is a tool that helps a project manager envision the fundamental components of a project plan. The more experienced you become, the less reliant you'll be on the vanilla methodology, which goes to the second point. A project management methodology can be used by a project manager of any experience level as a starting point and guide during the numerous planning stages.

- Less experienced project managers will stay a little closer to the methodology's detailed guidelines.
- More experienced project managers will use the methodology as one of several ingredients to a methodology of their own design that is tailored to the specific needs of the project.

This is a very important distinction.

> "A methodology is one of many ingredients used to *tailor* an approach that meets the unique needs of the client."

I love methodologies. In fact, I've developed a few myself. But methodologies, in the wrong hands, are also a little dangerous. You see, sometimes consultants and project managers let a methodology do the thinking for them. And when they do, they pick paths that are laid out in a form-supported phase of an approved methodology without giving the specific circumstances any consideration. This is bad.

One of the fundamental rules of project management is to meet the client and the circumstances where they are. This means you have to cast a wide net and learn about the drivers of the project. This includes:

- Outside political pressures;
- The external stakeholders and their expectations;
- The internal client executives and staff;
- The problems the project aims to solve; and
- Any mandatory deadlines outside of the organization's control.

Sure, you can use a methodology as a guide, but it won't be the go-to solution for everything you must account for in the plan.

> "Cast a wide net and learn about the drivers of the project."

Make sure the lens of a robust methodology isn't distorting or obscuring your view of the larger project context. And by robust, I mean a methodology that has been developed with unfettered enthusiasm for identifying every what-if scenario possible, one that might draw you into a bottom-

Belief 9: Effective Leaders Master the Material

less vortex of complexity, blurring the forest for the trees.

> "Don't subordinate your own observations, instincts, thinking, and analysis to the dictates of a methodology alone."

Bottom line, don't subordinate your own observations, thinking, gut instincts, and analysis to the dictates of a methodology alone.

The Methodology-Centric Crowd

There are a lot of methodology wonks out there in project management land. Be afraid. Be very afraid. They live and breathe their conceptual frameworks, holding tightly to their "right" answers. I've actually witnessed the "weaponization" of methodologies, used by the PMO chief to beat creative PMs into submission, common sense be damned! Left unrestrained, they will suck the life out of your efforts.

Now, to be clear, I'm not saying that it's acceptable for you as the project manager to forego developing a mastery of the conventional PM tools and techniques used to track project health. I'm saying this: to most non-PM types (i.e., your client), all the formulas and numbers are obscure, and when the focus of status reporting is too much on the number crunching, the status update experience often leaves them confused about what's really going on. And they're the ones who really need to know how the project is progressing.

Having a mastery of how to use PERT formulas to analyze schedules, Earned Value Analysis to calculate cost and schedule variances, or Expected Monetary Value in risk assessment is fine. You *should* be getting regular reports from the PMO staff once they've done their periodic number crunching. Those reports are a tool for you to use in managing the project; not the other way around. It's your job to review the implications of those reports, identify any deviations from plan and determine the root cause. They provide backup to your analysis and reports. Don't lead with them in an executive steering committee, and for that matter, your team meetings.

The Emerging Project Management Office

Around the early 2000s, when the Project Management standards body began rolling out methodological tools and techniques for planning and managing projects (and requiring certification in the same), it was common for organizations to establish a Project Management Office (PMO) as a means of compliance and establishing greater legitimacy. Hundreds, if not thousands of staff hours, were spent setting up complex project tracking systems capable of generating reports that could bring a tear to the eye of an aerospace engineer.

And the result? Well, I'm not sure, but I can tell you this. On countless occasions, I've walked into an executive's office where one corner of the desk was piled high with incredibly detailed spreadsheets and complicated diagrams. Someone from the PMO had been dutifully delivering those reports for weeks, and they'd been left untouched since.

I've listened to dozens of executive steering committee presentations from mid-level PMO staff running through a host of PM calculations without two things: 1) an explanation of why the numbers are relevant, and 2) a clear understanding of the larger project context.

It's not about the data alone. But the data, interpreted in context, can be of great value. If you use the data in your reporting, you must be able to explain the implications in a way that's *meaningful* and allows an executive or team leader to answer the following questions:

- What does this mean in terms of the work I'm responsible for?
- How does it fit into the larger effort?
- What specific actions do I need to take right now?

The project executives cannot manage what they cannot see. Like you, they can't see the root causes of current issues and understand why your solutions will work if the progress reporting system is muddied with extraneous details that seem important but don't really matter. You provide information that your client understands, that your team understands and feeds with updates, and that doesn't take a team of 20 people in a PMO office to maintain.

If you don't, you'll spend too much time wrestling with data while Nero fiddles.

PART V

FINAL THOUGHTS

BELIEF 10: COURAGEOUS LEADERS RUN TO THE ROAR

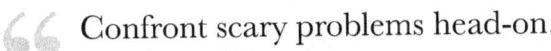 Confront scary problems head-on.

A few years ago, the pastor at our church shared a story about courage. It's a powerful story for this reason: it fundamentally changed the way I deal with the issues that trigger my fears and phobias.

The story is set on the beautiful continent of Africa, a land blessed with savannas, open tropical grasslands that provide food to grazing herds of animals, such as zebras or gazelles. You've seen the National Geographic programs, right? The views are breathtaking, and as the camera crew rides along the bumpy dirt roads, we watch in mesmerized awe … until.

Yes, I suspect you've watched the drama unfold too. First, there's the noise ... danger. And the herd, in a split second, turns in unison to run away.

And just as quickly, a lion comes into the camera's view, running at full speed to meet their prey.

Head on.

Wait ... head on? Wasn't the herd running *away* from the danger?

What happened here?

Well, the lions didn't just show up for lunch without a plan. They had a strategy, and a pretty clever one at that.

As the pride sets up the trap, the oldest members, now weak and toothless, are sent away from the younger and stronger lions. After all, the older lions are pretty useless. Except for one thing.

They can still roar.

So, they take their strategically selected place on a knoll opposite the grassy area where the younger members of the pride have gathered in the high grasses to hide.

As the grazing animals enter the area between the old toothless lions and the younger ones of the pride, the old lions start roaring, triggering a panic in the herd. Disoriented and afraid, the herd turns to flee the danger, running right to where the strongest lions are waiting for lunch to be served.

> "Run to the roar," say the elders to the young. When faced with great dangers in this world, run toward the roaring, go where you fear to go, for only there will you find some safety and a way through danger. Trouble that is faced when it first appears can be the roar that awakens a person's deepest resources. In times of trouble or tragedy, a person either steps into life more fully or else slips into a diminished life characterized by fear and anxiety.
>
> — Michael Meade, Why the World Doesn't End: Tales of Renewal in Times of Loss

I once found myself in a bit of a relational pickle. Weeks and months had gone by without so much as a peep from the person I was waiting to hear from. I wasn't happy about it. I felt ignored, and a little rejected. One day while sitting in the quiet of the backyard, I remembered this story. I decided I would do it. I would run to the roar (in this case, the roar of silence).

When I arrived for our chat, I was surprisingly relaxed. I had run to the roar; I was facing it down. In the process of talking it out, I discovered that the threat was really a toothless and hapless lion. It was invigorating! I was being true to myself, and I was pretty dang happy with myself. What an epiphany! The act of running towards the roar had actually changed me from someone easily duped by fears and anxiety into someone who was no longer afraid to face down the fear and expose the threat for what it truly was.

Now I know that 99% of the time, it's just a loud noise.

Awaken your deepest resources: when trouble or tragedy comes, run to the roar and step into your life more fully. You'll be better for it in all areas of your life.

NOTES

Belief 2: It's Always About the Path Forward

1. Timothy MacKenzie Gunn is an American fashion consultant, television personality, actor, voice actor and author. He served on the faculty of Parsons The New School for Design from 1982 to 2007 and was chair of fashion design at the school from August 2000 to March 2007, after which he joined Liz Claiborne as its chief creative officer. Over 16 seasons Gunn has become well known as the on-air mentor to designers on the reality television program Project Runway.**Wikipedia**

Belief 3: Integrity is King

1. **Cover your ass** (British: **arse**), abbreviated **CYA**, is activity done by an individual to protect themselves from possible subsequent criticism, legal penalties, or other repercussions, usually in a work-related or bureaucratic context. In one sense, it may be rightful steps to protect oneself properly while in a difficult situation, such as what steps to take to protect oneself after being fired.[1] But, in a different sense, according to *The New York Times*' language expert William Safire, it describes "the bureaucratic technique of averting future accusations of policy error or wrongdoing by deflecting responsibility in advance".[2] It often involves diffusing responsibility for one's actions as a form of insurance against possible future negative repercussions.[2] It can denote a type of institutional risk-averse mentality which works against accountability and responsibility, often characterized by excessive paperwork and documentation,[3] which can be

harmful to the institution's overall effectiveness.[4] The activity, sometimes seen as instinctive,[5] is generally unnecessary towards accomplishing the goals of the organization, but helpful to protect a particular individual's career within it, and it can be seen as a type of institutional corruption working against individual initiative.[6]

Belief 4: Leaders Are Ready to be Lightning Rods

1. I must offer a caveat to this principle. If you are the responsible manager of your firm's employees and encounter competency-related performance issues, it is typically your responsibility to work with the individual in developing and executing a performance improvement plan, complete with goals and timelines.

   However, this does not apply to staff employed by the client, or staff employed by other firms engaged on the project. If the project processes you've set up are working as designed, the need for a little HR intervention will become obvious. It's advisable to make your main client contact aware of any issues and let them take the issue forward to the appropriate manager.

Belief 6: Every Team Member is a Treasure

1. . The **forming–storming–norming–performing** model of group development was first proposed by Bruce Tuckman in 1965,[1] who said that these phases are all necessary and inevitable in order for the team to grow, face up to challenges, tackle problems, find solutions, plan work, and deliver results.
   https://en.wikipedia.org/wiki/Tuckman%27s_stages_of_group_development

If you would like to read an overview of the original four stages plus a fifth subsequently added, this link will take you to a pdf file that may be helpful.
   https://ess110.files.wordpress.com/2009/02/tuckmans_model.pdf
2. . https://en.wikipedia.org/wiki/Kindness
3. Here is a Forbes article on the topic of "how you say it." A great read.
   https://www.forbes.com/sites/adriandearnell/2018/07/10/its-not-what-you-say-its-how-you-say-it-why-perception-matters-when-presenting/#455502430adc

ENJOY THIS BOOK? YOU CAN MAKE A DIFFERENCE

If you've enjoyed this book I would be very grateful if you could spend just five minutes leaving a review (it can be as short as you like) on the book's product page. You can jump right to the page by clicking the link below or typing this address in your browser.

https://books2read.com/ten-things-believe

Leave my review

ALSO BY ...

BY SHANNON KUZMICH
Writing as Kathryn Wise

THE VAUGHN ALGORITHM

BY SHANNON KUZMICH

RESCUING CHRISTINA
A True Story About the Power of Love

PROJECT LEADERSHIP

The Ten Most Important Things You Need to Believe

PRESSING PLAY

Choosing the Path Forward After an Unexpected Pause

ABOUT THE AUTHOR

Shannon Kuzmich is an author who writes both fiction and nonfiction books while dabbling with design and animation on the side, all of this in between her newly inherited domestic duties and motherly obligations.

In her former life, before a portion of the family's domestic duties had been allocated to her plate, she worked in management and technology consulting, and did a pretty adequate job even if she does say so herself. She speaks and writes out of her experience of almost 35 years as both an internal consultant in the insurance, power utility, and telephony industries; and as an outside consultant with a variety of large, medium, and (her own) small consulting firms serving both public and private sector clients.

If you need more information, you can send her an email to request her 15-page resume at shannon@shannonkuzmich.com. She probably won't send it to you, but she'll be flattered by your interest. And no, she's not looking for a job.

Thanks for reading her little book. You've made her very happy.

facebook.com/AuthorShannonKuzmich